Keep the joy of life alive :

Jacqueline Thea

Also by the Author

Thea, Spiritual Midwife
New Meaning to Life after Death

Copyright 2010 by Jacqueline Thea, PhD
Published by Thea Associates, Bend, Oregon

Wake Up Your Fairy Grandmother Within!

You're Never Too Old to Be Young at Heart

Jacqueline Thea, PhD

BALBOA
PRESS
A DIVISION OF HAY HOUSE

Copyright © 2019 Jacqueline Thea, PhD.

Interior and Cover Credit: Vicki Shuck

All rights reserved. No part of this book may be used or reproduced by any means, graphic, electronic, or mechanical, including photocopying, recording, taping or by any information storage retrieval system without the written permission of the author except in the case of brief quotations embodied in critical articles and reviews.

Balboa Press books may be ordered through booksellers or by contacting:

Balboa Press
A Division of Hay House
1663 Liberty Drive
Bloomington, IN 47403
www.balboapress.com
1 (877) 407-4847

Because of the dynamic nature of the Internet, any web addresses or links contained in this book may have changed since publication and may no longer be valid. The views expressed in this work are solely those of the author and do not necessarily reflect the views of the publisher, and the publisher hereby disclaims any responsibility for them.

The author of this book does not dispense medical advice or prescribe the use of any technique as a form of treatment for physical, emotional, or medical problems without the advice of a physician, either directly or indirectly. The intent of the author is only to offer information of a general nature to help you in your quest for emotional and spiritual well-being. In the event you use any of the information in this book for yourself, which is your constitutional right, the author and the publisher assume no responsibility for your actions.

Print information available on the last page.

ISBN: 978-1-9822-2940-5 (sc)
ISBN: 978-1-9822-2939-9 (e)

Library of Congress Control Number: 2019907365

Balboa Press rev. date: 06/26/2019

What others are saying about—

Wake Up Your Fairy Grandmother Within: You're Never Too Old to Be Young at Heart

"Wow! What a delightful book, I shared this book with my 84 year old mom. She loved it too. Jacqueline Thea opens the doors to possibilities and wonder. As a former owner of an in home care agency working with seniors, two things were evident. One was that they didn't get touched enough, which is vital to thriving. And the second was that many lost connection with others as their world got smaller and smaller. Thea helps recreate a reason to delight in our aging process. She reminds us that love is something we can give and receive at any age; that our story is something important to share with others; and that our inner world is full of magic and insights to who we are. Life is so much bigger and better when we allow for magic. And the fairy grandmother is just that! I highly recommend this book to anyone who has forgotten that we came into this world full of wonder and curiosity and though we forgot that in our daily lives as adults, we can choose to leave this world with that same twinkle in our eye and that same appreciation in our hearts of life's greatest invention...ourselves."

—**Ali Davidson**, author, coach, counselor, facilitator/trainer

"I just finished reading *Wake Up Your Fairy Grandmother Within*. I couldn't put it down until I turned the last page. I found the stories to be inspirational and full of hope. Reading through the questions at the end of book I felt empowered. It made me think that no matter how different we think we are from one another we are so very much alike in our hopes and dreams. Thea shares the gift of her stories. I am excited to have my Fairy Grandmother Wake Up."

—**Brenda Chilcott**, Bend Senior Center Program Coordinator

"Jacqueline Thea's charming short stories were easy to read, kept my attention and made me think a lot about my own losses in life. I believe this would be a great resource for our residents to read together as a group and then continue with weekly group discussion. It would be a great way for our residents to share their thoughts and feelings in a safe environment; always coming back to something positive to add to their day. I look forward to the book being published and using it as a support group tool in our facility."

—**Rebecca Hankey**, Executive Director, Regency Village at Bend (A Retirement and Assisted Living Community)

"I thoroughly enjoyed the engaging *Wake Up Your Fairy Grandmother Within: You're Never Too Old to Be Young at Heart* with its delightful characters and their charming, teaching stories. The idea of a fairy grandmother lightened my heart and I look forward to gifting several of my clients with Jacqueline's book."

—**Belinda Ashenfelter**, Guardian/Conservator for senior adults

"Wow, what an insightful book, so moving. The stories deeply resonated within my own life stories to reflect upon my life path, the sorrows, challenges and eventual joy. No doubt, others will feel the same. I found the Readers Guide particularly helpful for 'processing'. The questions are well thought out and thought provoking. Bottom line, I loved the book and would definitely share the magic and joy with friends and family."

—**Nancy Webre**, MS, CMC Geriatric Care Manager. CEO/Owner Evergreen In-Home Care

*To all the grandmothers
in all the worlds*

Your Fairy Grandmother Within

Grants Your True Heart's Desire

The Gang of Three

Little Stories with Big Magic

> In the midst of winter, I found there was,
> within me, an invincible summer.
> —Albert Camus

What's Happening Inside?

Acknowledgments	xxi
Introduction	xxiii
My Grandma Mary Jo's Story	1
Your Fairy Grandmother Within	5
Prince, the Charming Greyhound	11
The Dandelion Fairy	21
Little Sunshine	29
After Thoughts	37
Your Fairy Grandmother's Wake-Up Call	45
Fairy Grandmother's Meditation	47
Reader's Guide	51
Resources	69
About the Author	71

In My Old Age

When I'm an old woman,
I shall put on fairy wings
And pick up my magic wand.
I will step into my power.

I shall spread the spark of joy,
I shall make your dreams come true,
I shall free the child within,
And I will sing,

"Fairy tales can come true
It can happen to you
If you're young at heart."
Hallelujah! I'll jump up and live again.

—Jacqueline Thea

> Storyteller's License
>
> This official license gives
>
> *Jacqueline Thea*
>
> permission to use her imagination in
> rearranging her experiences
> to improve a story, so long as it
> serves some notion of truth.

Imagination is the soil that brings dreams to life.
—Anonymous

Acknowledgments

Many people, pets, and circumstances in the physical and spiritual realms came together to help make my dream come true and give life to my fairy grandmother within.

First, I want to acknowledge the grandmothers who want all the worlds to be happy. Their empowerment sparked the fairy grandmother into my imagination and filled me with joy.

My appreciation to Sharon McErlane for sharing her inspiration and ongoing leadership of the Grandmothers' Council. Also, to the women who attended the Northern California Net of Light Gathering in 2018.

Thanks to Tricia O'Hara for providing me with the physical space and emotional support for the gestation and birthing of my bundle of joy. Gratitude to Belinda Ashenfelter, insightful editor and special friend. Susan Stafford offered discerning advice. Barbara Schnell, Su Skjersaa, and Ellie Waterston gave suggestions and ongoing encouragement. Special kudos to Karen Anagnost, who socked it to me with her truth. Maria Wattier and our dream group continue to provide added value to my dreams. You all are prized.

Blessings to my daughter, Candace Gomber Brey, and

surrogate daughter, Nancy Beckley, for listening and caring. Your love continues to be essential.

Admiration to Vicki Shuck, whose enchanted illustrations gave life to my friends.

Appreciation to all those at Balboa Press who helped give feet and wings to my dream.

A special tribute to my beloved Prince, the charming greyhound, who lives in my heart; to the Dandelion Fairy, who keeps me young at heart; and to Little Sunshine, who finally found healing and speaks from my soul. And a nod to sweet Sophia.

Introduction

There is nothing as dangerous as an old woman on fire!

One glorious autumn day in 2018, a fairy grandmother sprang forth in my imagination and sparked joy in my life. At the time, my soul ached with grief from the recent passing of Prince, my beloved greyhound and longtime companion. Just five days before, I held his regal but worn-out body as his spirit slowly crossed the Rainbow Bridge. His loss left a hole in my soul.

The enchanting emergence of my fairy grandmother occurred at a gathering of about fifty women who came together to celebrate the power of the sacred feminine and share their concerns for the plight of the planet, our Mother Earth. In my grief, I almost didn't attend.

As we gathered in small groups to share our personal experiences, I wept, speaking of my sorrow in losing my beloved companion. The group leader told me she could actually sense the presence of Prince in the room, but all I sensed was my loss.

Later, all the women stood to receive an empowering blessing. We placed our hands on each other's shoulders and in prayer, asked the loving spirits of older women to bless us and grant our true hearts' desires. As I received my blessing, a radiant lifelike figure, surrounded in a luminous aura, came out of nowhere and floated above my head. Although unable to see her face, I felt the effects of her magic wand. She was my fairy grandmother.

My grief seemed to melt. Deep within, the presence of my precious Prince began to stir. Joy filled the hole in my soul. My true heart's desire had been granted. Prince had come home to live in my heart. My dark night of sorrow transformed into a new day. I felt so alive. Just like Dorothy in *The Wizard of Oz*, when Glinda, the good witch, magically appeared, I wanted to click my heels together and dance.

When I heard the leader say, "Pass on the blessing," I knew that the right vehicle had arrived for me. I believed that most people would love to be touched by a magic wand and experience their true hearts' desires. I could do this. I wanted the whole world to be happy. The inspiration fired my imagination!

Envisioning a new mission in my old age, I imagined myself dressing up as the fairy grandmother, carrying my magic wand to spark joy, and sprinkling a little fairy dust around senior centers, retirement communities, and assisted living facilities. Woohoo!

During my career in the helping professions, I began as a nurse's aide and later studied to become a registered nurse. As a vocational rehabilitation counselor, I assisted clients with disabilities to return to work. For many years as a professional guardian and conservator appointed by the courts, I protected incapacitated persons, especially seniors with disabilities, mostly women. As a volunteer with several hospice organizations, I sat with the dying and offered emotional support to their families. I knew what difficulties aging and life could bring in its wake.

Having slow danced through a few sorrows of my own, I knew the territory. In 2009, I had lost my supportive, loving husband. In 2013, my oldest son, who had turned his life around after his drug rehabilitation, died from complications of hepatitis C. In 2018, my youngest son lingered near death following a three-day coma and continues to suffer the aftereffects. Also in that year, I lost two precious cats in addition to Prince, my beloved dog. But life still held magic. Having felt this joy of discovery, I wanted to share the inspiring world of enchantment with others.

Where to begin? I wondered. *How would the fairy grandmother introduce herself into the community? What would she say? What would people think? Should she go to schools where young children still believed in fairies? Could she suddenly appear at the door of a senior center or in the halls of a nursing home with her magic wand and say, "I'm here to spark joy and grant your heart's desire"? Some people might think her crazy or call the cops and lock her up.*

A dilemma!

An idea popped. Aha! The fairy grandmother needed a hook! She couldn't just wander into this world alone. She needed companions with inspiring stories to tell. Since I had a Storyteller's License, I could write a book from my own life experiences! I could tell the story of Prince, my charming greyhound, and his connection to the miraculous appearance of the fairy grandmother in my life. A book would make the whole story legitimate.

Then the Dandelion Fairy, an outrageously funny little fairy who wanted to be the star of the Pixie Circus, came to mind because she reminded me of the cute little kid who lived inside me and always wanted to show off and be the star. The story of the Dandelion Fairy could join Prince in my book.

The epiphany continued.

I remembered Little Sunshine, another part of my inner world. I called her my wounded soul child. The exciting story of her healing would be another great addition.

The book would introduce the fairy grandmother and her companions, her gang of three—Prince, the charming greyhound who crossed the Rainbow Bridge and returned; a hotshot, funny Dandelion Fairy who wanted to show off; plus a sad Little Sunshine, a wounded soul child who hid in my heart. I knew their magical tales would touch many people, especially lonely older women who suffered loss, disappointment, or depression. The book's bits of wisdom could spark joy, transform grief, give hope, and stir healing.

These stories are based on my own life experiences. If someone asked, "Is the fairy grandmother real?" I'd answer with another question: "Is joy real?" You can't *see* it, but you can certainly *feel* it.

I believe in two kinds of reality—ordinary reality and nonordinary reality. Ordinary reality includes the physical senses—seeing, hearing, tasting, touching, and smelling. Nonordinary reality transcends the physical senses. It includes the spiritual realms and dreamtime, where we see and hear with our inner eyes and ears. I walk between these worlds of reality.

I believe we all have an inner world, which can be referred to as the imaginary world or the imagination. Our inner world waits to be explored.

I believe we all have an inner child, a part of the self that remains in our inner world even as we age and mature. This part of our personality, formed in our early development, continues to influence our behavior as adults. The inner child, and there may be more than one, is sometimes called the magical child, divine child, or soul child. This child holds our trust and innocence, still believes in Santa Claus and fairies, and may have imaginary friends.

I believe we all have a delightful spirit of joy within who

anxiously awaits to wake up and make us happy. This spirit of joy is your fairy grandmother.

I believe we all carry our own personal stories that call for remembering. My heart's desire is that telling my stories will help readers remember and tell their stories.

In order to access the many dimensions and layers that might lay hidden in these childlike tales, this book—*Wake Up Your Fairy Grandmother Within!*—offers different ways to discover and utilize its many bits of wisdom. "Your Fairy Grandmother's Wake-Up Call" will help readers recognize their own fairy grandmothers and discover their own inner worlds. The imagination opens a whole new exciting realm to explore. "The Fairy Grandmother's Meditation" encourages readers to go within and expand their own inner wisdom. "The Reader's Guide" proposes questions for personal reflection and/or group discussion. Readers are also encouraged to remember and give life to their own stories. Since residents in retirement or assisted living facilities often find themselves alone and/or lonely, these questions can encourage conversation, group discussion, comradery, and storytelling.

In addition, I decided to share a story about my own grandma, Mary Jo. I loved that no-nonsense, hardworking farm woman with a big heart. As a child, while visiting my grandma on the farm, I heard her complaining about the chickens. "Grandma," I said, "if the chickens bother you so much, why don't you get rid of them?" Shaking her head, she replied, "Sakes alive, child, a body's got to have something to fuss at."

My plain-talking and plain-living grandma understood life at a basic level. With her down-to-earth wisdom, she had a way of comforting souls at the end of life and acted as spiritual midwife when it was time to pass on.

It is so important to remember our ancestors; "To remember is to give life." Surprisingly, we may be more connected than we know. My grandma's remarkable gift passed on to me, and that's one reason I share her story.

Although not young in age, I am still young at heart and want to share my fairy grandmother's heartfelt joy with other "seasoned citizens" who, like myself, are living in the autumn or winter of their lives. Some of us may feel old and cranky at times, others may suffer loss or disappointment, while still others are lonely or bored. For those who want to make contact with the playful parts of themselves, it is time to wake up your fairy grandmother! We all need a little joy to help celebrate life now, while we can. Yahoo!

Welcome to the realm of enchantment. May your fairy grandmother jump up and live again, shower you with magic fairy dust, and grant your true heart's desire!

My Grandma Mary Jo's Story

It was in the dead of night in the early 1900s on a farm in the hills of Tennessee. A lantern could be seen swinging in the dark as John, the neighbor with a sick wife, trudged through the fields to the farmhouse, calling, "Mary Jo, Mary Jo, we need you."

Mary Jo's sleepy-eyed children woke up and strained to listen.

"Sakes alive, I'm coming," Mary Jo called back. As her callused feet moved from the warm featherbed to the cold floor, she murmured to herself, "I know'd a crossin' to be near."

"I'll be back later," she told George as she grabbed a lantern from the nearby table and fumbled with the wick. "Don't fuss. The girls will cook the grits." Mary Jo threw a shawl around her shoulders.

When the porch door slammed, the children whispered to each other, "Someone must be dyin'. They always come for Mama."

Mary Jo had an unusual gift. She could walk between the worlds of ordinary and nonordinary reality. When it was time, she guided departing souls on their journeys home. She was a spiritual midwife. Mary Jo had the sight and could see the life-light flicker and then dim before a person passed on. And if you looked closely at her hands, you would notice the short and stubby thumbs that could almost double as big toes, genetically passed down on the female side. Some people called them "fairy thumbs," although Mary Jo would have considered that nonsense.

But maybe fairy blood could account for Mary Jo's sight, along with her thumbs. Some people claim that fairies do have magical powers, and the fairy thumbs may have come with the Celtic Scots-Irish blood that pulsed through Grandma's veins. One never really knew about these mysteries. The Celts had a tradition called *Anam Cara,* Gaelic for "soul friend." Grandma seemed to live that tradition. As a friend of the soul, she could sit with the dying as they made their transitions and give comfort to the living.

Mary Jo bore ten children. In 1913, Berta arrived, the seventh-born child. Mary Jo called her Bertie, and indeed, she was a beauty. Bertie came with the fairy thumbs passed from her mother, flaming red hair from her father, and a love of playing and dancing (maybe that came from the fairies). But she didn't receive the gift of Anam Cara or the ability to walk between worlds. That gift passed on to her daughter.

Your Fairy Grandmother Within

Wake Up Your Fairy Grandmother Within!

*Y*our fairy grandmother within will appear when you are ready. You are probably moving on in life with a few gray hairs; that is, if you don't color them. That's okay too. Your fairy grandmother keeps you young at heart. You get to choose how the outside looks!

You may have fulfilled your life plan or purpose, or not. Did you get to finish college or give it up to raise a family? Did your dream career find fulfillment? Did you take that longed-for adventure? Did your marriage or your children disappoint you? You may have wanted more and settled for less, but now those things don't matter. Savor them or let them go. Whatever makes you happy. Your fairy grandmother wants you to be happy.

You matter!

You may have known your fairy grandmother as a child but don't remember her now. Having grown older, you have survived many years, possibly a few bad ones along with the good. You may have discovered a bad egg or two in your carton. Your heart may have suffered several cracks or even been broken as loved ones, friends, or special pets found their wings, and you weren't ready to let them go. You may still carry that grief.

You are never too old to be young at heart. You are aged to perfection! You can now claim your own fairy grandmother. She is the spirit within every person that seeks to spark joy. That spirit carries special medicine to transform grief, give hope, and stir healing.

Your fairy grandmother may be sleeping, waiting for your nudge, or knocking at your heart's door. She may look like a special loved one or your grandmother. She may be a heavenly vision with wings and a magic wand. She may be a revelation or even look like a whimsical cartoon character.

What? You don't believe me? You think that's just for others, not for you? "I don't have a spirit of joy inside me," you say. "If I did, it dried up long ago."

Don't believe it! That's just the bad egg talking. The spirit of joy—your fairy grandmother within—is enchanted. She radiates eternal light. You may not have the eyes to see, but trust me. Your fairy grandmother is like a star, but as with a star, you don't always see her. She's there. You'll see her when you least expect it. Maybe in a dream (look for the magic wand) or in your mirror (she may resemble you).

"I'm here for you," says your fairy grandmother. "I'm waiting to spark joy in your life." Your fairy grandmother is speaking to you. Listen to her!

You may think you're too old to believe in fairy tales, but you'll always be my own sweet child—my bundle of joy. You may not believe in me, but I believe in you. I am your fairy grandmother. This is my gift to you! Believe!

Stories

To remember is to give life.

Prince, the Charming Greyhound

*P*rince, the charming greyhound, is a magnificent, handsome specimen of royal dignity, a racer who retired with honors from a greyhound track in Miami, Florida, where he was known as Gettin' Ahead. Greyhound dogs are trained to run and win. No one loves them or even treats them in a special way. Gettin' Ahead won many races but never had a real home or friends.

Gettin' Ahead raced until he was almost six years old. That's a long time for a greyhound to race. When he retired, he went to Florida Bay Area Greyhound Adoptions, where they called him Frankie and selected him for the Second Chance at Life Greyhound Prison Program, held at the Gadsden Correctional Institution, a women's prison in north Florida. His handler got a chance to learn a new skill; she learned how to train a dog. Frankie got a chance to learn some new tricks. He learned how to sit and stay and follow orders. He even learned to walk up and down stairs. Frankie learned how to be what people called a "good dog." Best of all for Frankie, he found someone to love him. Mary, his lady handler, had been lonely and longed for someone to love, and she showered that love on Frankie. He responded in kind. They became buddies, but it didn't last.

The program ended in nine weeks, and Frankie had to leave. He didn't understand. His heart ached because he missed Mary. He didn't know it, but an older couple, Ben and Margie, had been waiting for Frankie to finish his training and brought him to his new home, a small apartment in Miami, Florida. They all got acquainted. Ben wasn't well and spent a lot of time in bed. Margie loved Frankie and took him for long walks. He liked that. He settled in. After a few months, some men came and took

Ben away on a stretcher. Margie cried. She decided to move to a retirement community, but they didn't allow big dogs. Margie cried. Frankie didn't understand. Again, his heart ached.

Frankie then went to another home, this time a big house with a fenced yard and a new lady named Sue. She had another greyhound called Guy and even a cat named Pussy. They all got along, but Frankie kept to himself. He liked to sleep most of the time. Frankie hoped he could stay. He didn't know it was a foster home, a temporary place to live.

About this time, across the country in a state called Oregon, an older lady wanted an older dog for a companion. She decided to adopt a retired greyhound. The Greyhound Pet Adoption Northwest people matched her with Frankie, and those wonderful people drove all the way across the country to retrieve him. Frankie didn't know what was happening when he left his foster home and jumped into a covered trailer. Two people, a woman and a man, took turns driving the truck that pulled the big trailer. The woman slept while the man drove, and then they traded off. During the long ride, they made two more stops to pick up more greyhounds. Other than that, they only stopped to eat and pee. Since greyhounds had never learned to play, they didn't interact. Frankie slept most of the time.

After several days, they arrived in Oregon. Frankie shivered in the cold when he finally jumped out of the trailer. He wasn't in Florida anymore. Another man and woman helped unload the trailer and welcomed them home. Frankie just shook his head in wonder, but the nice gray-haired man treated him well and scratched his ears. He let the dogs run around for a while in the yard. Later he put Frankie in a place called the Hounds Rest, a big garage with lots of crates. Frankie rested.

The next afternoon, the nice man took Frankie to live in a real house with a fenced yard. The lady named Joy seemed glad to see Frankie and gave him a hug. He hoped this could be his forever home. Frankie grew wary when Joy took him to the dog doctor, called a "vet." The vet looked in his mouth and gave him shots. Frankie fell asleep, and they cleaned his teeth. After he returned to the house, he wondered what would happen next.

Several days later, Frankie was doing his business in the yard when he saw a car drive up, and another lady got out. She came in and talked to Joy, who gave the lady a leash and some papers to sign. Joy told her what a good dog Frankie had been.

"Come on, Frankie," the new lady said. "Jump up in the car. I'm your new owner, and we're going home." Frankie wondered what the word "home" really meant. The car looked small, but the backseat went flat, and with lots of blankets, it made a nice bed. Frankie settled down. They started driving over the mountain. The new lady stopped at a store and reassured him that she would be right back. She brought him a big doggie biscuit and scratched his ears. He liked that. Later, she stopped again to let him pee. They arrived in a town called Bend and pulled into a small garage. Before Frankie could jump out of the car, his new lady attached his leash to make sure he didn't run away. Greyhounds are trained to run, and they run fast! And Frankie was a grade-A racer.

"Welcome home," his new lady said. Frankie wondered

if this was just another stop along the way. He didn't trust anyone. Frankie looked around warily. He smelled cats, more than one. He didn't mind cats if they didn't bother him. The lady showed him through the big house and pointed to his beds, one in the front room and one in her bedroom. She lived alone. Although suspicious, Frankie was tired. He lay down on the bed in the front room, where he could keep an eye on this new lady.

Remembering other times, Frankie couldn't look directly in her eyes and connect because he thought she might leave him or give him back. Whenever this new lady left the house, he got nervous and peed on the carpet. She got upset, but she talked kindly to him and didn't scold. One day, she gently held his head and pressed her forehead next to his. Finally, Frankie looked in her eyes. Peace. They connected. "You're a regal, handsome dog," she said. "I'll call you Prince. You are my Prince Charming." Prince decided to call her My Lady.

Frankie became Prince, his new forever name, and his wish came true. He finally found his forever home. He wants to tell you the rest of the story.

My Story

My name is Prince, I lived a long time in my forever home with My Lady, my friend and companion. She took me with her everywhere—to the store, parties, meetings, even to the hairdresser! I learned to trust that whenever she left me, she would always return. We had a happy life. My Lady bought me toys and bones and took me to the dog park every day. I ran with other dogs, and even though I never learned to play, I got to sniff and pee. As I pranced through the park, people would say, "What a regal dog," and then pet me. I loved to have my ears rubbed.

My Lady knew I was a gentle soul. The only time I barked was when two dogs began to fight. At least it looked to me like they were fighting. I barked to break them up. My Lady called me the Sheriff of Ponderosa Dog Park. One has to understand that a gentle soul does not like to see a fight.

I kept my racing weight at around seventy-five pounds and looked sleek even though some people called me skinny. My black coat went a little gray, but I stood strong and tall. In our time together, we made visits to the beach. My Lady loved the ocean waves, and I loved walking on the sand. We stayed in a motel room on the first floor, so I didn't have to climb the stairs. I don't like to climb stairs, and My Lady was thoughtful that way. In the morning, she'd leave for a while. I'd be anxious, but she'd return with a tray of food. She always brought me a peanut butter cup. What a treat! I loved licking peanut butter from those little cups. That made me happy. Sometimes we'd stroll on the boardwalk to look at the seals. They made such funny noises. She laughed. I peed on the bushes. We made a handsome couple. People would stop us to ask, "Is that a greyhound? How wonderful you rescued him." She told my story and always said, "He's such a gentle soul."

My Lady gave me the forever home that I always longed for. She loved me with a great love that made my heart glad to be alive. The nice way she treated me, her tone of voice, the way she hugged me and felt so proud. It made me proud as well. My Lady bought two more beds, one to put in the kitchen and one in her office. Wherever my friend sat or stood, I wanted to be nearby. I loved that lady.

We had more than six years together before my age caught up with me, and my rear parts began to fail. I lost feeling in my back legs, and they began to tremble. When I could no longer jump into the car, we had to quit the dog park. My Lady couldn't lift me, and I didn't like to climb up the steep ramp. Then one day as we were walking, I stumbled on the stairs, and we both fell. I knew the time had come. Danger lurked ahead; it made me sad. I let my companion know that we weren't safe. My Lady understood. She cried. The next day she reluctantly made a phone call. Her voice trembled as she invited someone to come to our home.

That afternoon, the lady vet came. The two ladies talked. My Lady told the vet lady the story of my life and how much she loved me. The vet lady agreed that I was a prize. My Lady got down on the floor and held my head in her lap while the vet lady gently poked me. The cats, Alice and Megan, lay nearby. We had become friends. I relaxed, and the pain in my backside disappeared. I looked one last time in My Lady's eyes, and I could see her tears. As I fell asleep, I heard the vet lady say, "He had a strong heart." My spirit slowly crossed the Rainbow Bridge. I did not look back.

A big surprise awaited on the other side—a world full of light with angels and music, nice people to pet me, lots of trees to sniff, green grass for running, other dogs to chase, lots of treats, no cats. It seemed like the best dog park ever. They called it heaven. My running legs felt strong again. The pain was gone, and my gray hair disappeared. A new life force filled me.

Then I found the most wonderful secret of all. A

beautiful lady who looked like an angel whispered in my ear, "Our love is our power." In heaven, love is bigger and better than anything else; love makes all things possible. Heaven allows us to travel back and forth across the Rainbow Bridge to visit our loved ones and friends in their hearts and in their dreams. Not everyone can see us. However if they tried hard, they might feel us in their hearts. When I discovered that love is stronger than death, my ears perked up. I raced back across the Rainbow Bridge to take a bit of this heaven to My Lady. I returned to live in her heart. Now we are both happy.

Until one has loved an animal, a part of one's soul remains unawakened.

—-Anatole France

The Dandelion Fairy

Story ideas adapted from the *Pixie Circus* by Molly Brett.

*T*his delightful tale about the Dandelion Fairy and the Pixie Circus is one that will appeal to your inner child, that cute little kid within who never grew up. You might recognize this impish, funny fairy right away. Did you ever like to show off or want to be the center of attention? If you did, it may have caused you considerable consternation more often than you'd like to admit. But it's hard not to smile at that inner scalawag. She loves to play and is always so full of hope and joy.

This fairy tale shares her excitement and enthusiasm for life. Let the Dandelion Fairy connect with your inner child. She loves to have fun.

Once upon a springtime day in the enchanted land of Faerie, the Pixies, who lived in a big wildflower field, began planning a circus after the long, cold winter had passed.

The ringmaster, Tufty Tail the squirrel, watched Pipkin the elf, Fuzzy the hedgehog, Flop the frog, Midget the mouse, and Old Mole as they practiced their acts and played their music. In the center of the ring, riding her rabbit, the Dandelion Fairy practiced hardest of all because she wanted to be the first act and open the circus.

The Dandelion Fairy wants to tell her own story. So let her speak to your inner child.

My Story

I'm the Dandelion Fairy. I became so excited about being in the Pixie Circus that my wings tingled, making me laugh. I practiced every day, dancing on the back of my rabbit, whom I called Speedy. We raced round and round in the wildflower field. I do love springtime. After all, I am a Dandelion Fairy.

All the circus performers practiced together in a big circle on the grass. The clown, Fuzzy the hedgehog, practiced turning somersaults. He also juggled berries and did other special tricks. Fuzzy made quite a good clown. He wore a funny, big, white hat with a red ball on the top. He had a white fluffy collar around his neck to match. He made people laugh.

Off to the side, the band kept busy rehearsing their music. Old Mole, who was rather deaf, banged his drum too loudly and not always in the right place. When Flop the frog and Midget the mouse asked him to keep in time, Old Mole grew grumpy and banged even louder. I wondered if he would make trouble.

I practiced hard because I wanted to be the headline star of the circus. But the ringmaster, Tufty Tail the squirrel, decided to open the show with Pipkin the elf walking a tightrope with his two pet butterflies. Although some of my best friends are elves—and I think they are cute and all, especially Pipkin—but I had way more pizzazz than him.

I sulked a little because I had the best act and wanted to be first. I told the ringmaster my ideas, but he didn't change his mind. I stomped my foot and walked away. I think he worried a bit about what I might do.

At last, the big day arrived. A large group of birds, mice, frogs, rabbits, and other animals, plus the elves and fairies who lived in the forest, came out and gathered around in the ring of daises to watch the circus. The band began to play. I hugged Speedy and whispered in his big ear, "Wait and see. We'll be the stars."

As planned, Pipkin, looking perky in his red shirt, blue shorts, and a feather in his cap, walked gingerly across the grass stem balanced by his two big, beautiful butterflies. The audience clapped loudly. But they hadn't seen me yet. I waited on the sidelines.

Surprise! Without further ado, dancing on the back of Speedy, my rabbit, I dashed into the center of the ring carrying a bouquet of flowers. Looking quite stunning in green satin with a yellow tutu and matching slippers, I tossed my red curls and threw flowers to the surprised audience. Jumping from one foot to the other and fluttering my iridescent wings, I cried, "Watch me and my fast rabbit. We should have been first!" My wings shimmered in the sunlight. We made quite a spectacular show.

We went round and round the ring while everyone clapped. This upset the befuddled ringmaster. In a quandary, Tufty didn't know what to do. He couldn't stop me. Fuzzy the clown kept juggling his berries; he's rather good. Pipkin the elf kept walking the tightrope; he has exceptional balance. But nobody noticed them now. Everyone looked at me. I became the star of the Pixie Circus. Throwing my arms high in the air, I laughed and relished the cheering from the crowd. Then, swirling around, I bowed.

Finally, Old Mole realized something unusual was happening. He grunted and yelled at me, "You're out of your turn, you conceited thing!" Angrily, he gave his drum a big thump—*Bom! Bom!* He frightened my rabbit.

"Oh no," I cried. Speedy jumped so high in the air that

I fell off his back. Someone once said, "Pride goes before a fall." I fell.

Crash! I landed right in the center of Old Mole's drum! That wasn't in the plan. The audience gasped and didn't know whether to laugh or applaud. I cried.

Sad to say, I did not get the admiration I expected. And I also lost Speedy; he ran away. And Old Mole couldn't play his drum anymore because it had a big hole in it. Although Pipkin kept walking on the blade of grass with his butterflies, the Pixie Circus did not have a happy ending.

I picked myself up, dusted myself off, and told the confused ringmaster that it was all the Old Mole's fault, and I deserved another chance. Looking bewildered, he shook his head sadly and told me, "We'll see what happens next year."

The Dandelion Fairy believes that it is better to have tried and failed than never to have tried at all. She also believes, "Hope triumphs over experience." So watch for her at next year's Pixie Circus. Surely, she and Speedy will return!

Everyone has a childlike spirit deep inside, maybe more than one. There are many kinds of childlike spirits, each unique in its own way. Some child spirits just love to play, some are lonely, some are afraid. Other child spirits have been hurt and hide. Some are just shy and need coaxing. Others are bold, and like the Dandelion Fairy, they sometimes crash. Those special ones need a hand to hold.

The Dandelion Fairy now travels with the fairy grandmother, ready to sprinkle fairy dust on all those who wish to be young at heart. She invites your childlike spirit to come out and play.

Little Sunshine

*M*y name is Little Sunshine. I know there are brave and bold child spirits like the Dandelion Fairy who laugh and play or long to be a star in the circus. Even when she falls, she is ready to get up and try again. People may be more in touch with that fun inner child. I'm a different kind of child spirit and have a different tale to tell. I'm connected to what is called the "soul," the spiritual part or the deep feelings of a person. Quite often these emotions are hidden. Most of my life I've been hiding and couldn't be seen or heard. Let me share my story, and listen with the ears of your inner child.

My Story

I call myself Little Sunshine. This is quite ironic because most of the time, I feel sad. But it makes me feel glad to think of sunshine. I live deep in my mommy's heart, where she stores her pain and tears. I am her soul child.

For many years, I tried talking to my mommy, but she never listened. Maybe she didn't recognize my voice or didn't want to hear. I remember bad dreams of being locked up by a witch and trying to escape, but I got caught. Then the angels came to my rescue. I wanted to tell mommy my dreams because they had a happy ending. I always hope for a happy ending. She didn't hear me.

It took a long, long time, but one day she heard my silent cry, the voice of her troubled deep feelings that finally found expression. She listened. I'll save that moment to share later. You'll be glad to know our story has a happy ending.

Since I'm a soul child, I live in my mommy's heart and have been with her since before she was even born, when she was still in her mommy's tummy. Those were hard times.

When her daddy heard a baby was coming, he ran away. My mommy's mom, I'll call her mom-mom, felt ashamed, afraid, and alone. Those feelings transferred to the baby. Mom-mom got scared and tried to send us away. We refused to go, but it hurt me. We weren't wanted.

My mommy's daddy finally came back and married Mom-mom. They made a family, but they did not live happily ever after. That's another story. As my mommy grew up, she still felt ashamed, afraid, and alone, but she ignored her sad feelings. My mommy's brave and tough, and she promised herself not to cry. She shut away her feelings, but they had to go someplace. Deep inside her heart, I felt the pain and held the tears. She learned how to play let's pretend. She learned the lesson well. I stayed hidden deep in her heart.

Mommy grew up, got married, and had a family of her own. Because she didn't feel loved, she had a hard time loving others. Her heart hurt, but she ignored the pain; the wounds left me scarred. I cried, but she didn't hear me.

A long time passed.

My mommy began to feel the wounds inside and sought ways to heal. She went to school and studied psychology; she found a psychotherapist and told her story. She heard people talk about the hurt and lonely inner child. She went to workshops where people told their stories and shared ways to heal. She began to see the inner world. She began to hear my faint voice. She found when the heart holds hurt, it also holds healing, and a whole new world opened—the spiritual world.

She studied shamanism and learned to travel between the physical and spiritual worlds to the beat of a drum, a sound reminiscent from the womb. She found the lower and upper realms, where she met spirit animals and spirit teachers. In the middle realm, she discovered the restless souls of the departed who needed help. She met her ancestors. My mommy realized she had her grandma Mary Jo's special gift, and she helped restless souls move on to the light. She even wrote a book called, *Thea, Spiritual Midwife— New Meaning to Life after Death.* My mommy also came to embrace the love of the Divine Mother. That made her very happy and is another story. But I still remained hidden in her heart, behind a wall of unshed tears. I waited.

A long time passed.

My mommy grew older and honored herself as a crone, a woman of age, wisdom, and power. She became a grandmother. She forgot about me. I waited.

A long time passed.

Her older son became ill and then crossed the Rainbow Bridge. She couldn't cry. I felt frozen. I loved her son; our souls resonated. I longed for her to express our sorrow. Her son returned in troubled dreams. He acted mad, and she asked his forgiveness. Then, my mommy attended a seminar with hospice nurses who helped troubled veterans find peace before they died by healing their soul injury—owning their guilt, forgiving themselves, and learning to mourn their losses. During the seminar, my mommy truly listened and finally heard the message. That wall of unshed tears came tumbling down. At last, my mommy learned how to mourn her loss. She grieved for her son; she grieved for herself.

Time passed.

One day, my mommy made a pilgrimage to Spain to

meet the spirits of her ancestors and to honor the land from where they came. She found a big surprise!

She found that Spain harbors a sorrowful spirit called *duende*. It is said duende came with the Gypsies when they settled in the south of Spain many years ago. Duende is a spirit of grief that comes from years of not being seen, valued, or wanted, of feeling "less than," feeling not only rejection but invisible. This mysterious life force troubles the ground of one's being. It is a power connected to anguish, mystery, and death. Duende inspires the flamenco dancers and singers, and it possesses poets who then write with their tears.

The immortal Spanish poet Federico Garcia Lorca personally knew the power of duende. Although he died tragically at the age of thirty-eight during the Spanish Civil War, in his lifetime, Lorca wrote about duende, lectured about duende, and referred to duende as the "pain that has no explanation, yet it is the source of much great art." My mommy visited Lorca's historical home, and his lingering presence touched her. She read his poignant poetry, and the spirit of duende begin to stir inside her.

Before the pilgrimage, my mommy had bought some flamenco dancing shoes and took a few lessons, attempting to connect with the passion that inspired the music. But it didn't work. While in Spain, she determined to connect with the real flamenco artists.

Disappointed after attending one flamenco performance, because it was just that, a performance for the tourists, she found another venue. This time she sat at the edge of the stage, where the enchantment of the dancers and musicians surrounded and captured her.

Those dancers and singers must have been possessed by

the spirit of duende because their performance transformed from ordinary to extraordinary. The female dancers stomped and spun, their brightly colored dresses swirled, their eyes flashed, and their raised arms moved in rhythm with their clicking fingers, tempting the male dancers who responded in kind. The dancers and musicians seemed lost in their own world, communicating with the beat of their feet and the pulse of their music.

The voice of the male singers cried out in despair. They sang not with pleasure but with pathos. Their songs opened wounds. They did not perform; they bared their souls.

My mommy listened not only with her ears but her heart, awakening the deep passion within. She not only witnessed the performance; she embraced it.

In the land of her ancestors, when that powerful spirit of duende touched my mommy's heart, a miracle happened! She heard her own soul's deep sorrow; she heard me. I had waited so long to be heard, I had almost given up hope. But this land of our ancestors held both the hurt and the healing. Through the years, I lived with hidden hurt. When my pain was finally heard, I discovered what it meant to be healed: "To be heard is to be healed."

Hallelujah! I jumped up to live again. Joy threw her arms around me in a big bear hug. I found my voice. My childlike spirit sprang forth to dance and sing.

"I am free. Free at last! Free to be happy. Free to run and play. Free to be me." My spirit soared. It is never too late to live again!

There are no words. The language falters when trying to convey the explosive feeling expressed by a soul set free from a concealed existence. Little Sunshine, that lonely little soul child within, personifies the lost part of my soul, now retrieved. Welcome home!

It is a gift of old age that allows enough time and enough water to wash under the bridge, to clear out the psychological debris and wake up the spirit of joy that allows us to live out our lives in peace.

Little Sunshine Rocks!

After Thoughts

*A*fter writing these little stories and then looking back with introspection, I wondered about the timing of the appearance of my fairy grandmother and the sequence of events.

The first story about Prince crossing the Rainbow Bridge and then returning to live in my heart happened after the healing of Little Sunshine, when her deep sorrow was finally heard. It occurred to me that one has to learn how to mourn loss, has to *feel* the anguish of a broken heart, in order for that pain to be transformed into bliss. As with a butterfly struggling to emerge from its dark cocoon, it seems one has to dwell in the shadows, to be touched by grief, before the fairy grandmother within—the spirit of joy—can awaken.

Oh, the paradox of this human existence.

I wondered if my fairy grandmother would have appeared to me if I hadn't gone to the Women's Gathering. Or was her appearance connected to that group? In my grief, I made the effort to connect with other women; we honored the sacred feminine spirit in the earth and within each other. We shared our blessings by connecting hearts and hands.

The fairy grandmother didn't appear out of nowhere. She appeared when I received a blessing and was told to "Pass it on." One way we pass on love to each other is by touch. It may be a warm handshake, a more personal hug, or a loved one's kiss. It may be the laying on of hands by a healer or priest, or the touch of a magic wand.

We can do this for each other. When we receive a blessing, we can pass it on. We can become a conduit of spiritual power similar to an electrical cord plugged into the source. In my case, that source of power took the form of a fairy grandmother—a simple, whimsical idea, an image of delightful joy—an enchanted, beloved being with a magic wand to grant my true heart's desire.

When the fairy grandmother sprang into my life, she transformed my grief into joy. Prince, my beloved greyhound, came home to live in my heart. When another person cared enough to reach out and pass on the blessing of love to me. I was ready to receive it.

My way of passing on this blessing includes writing this book and sharing my enchanting experience. I hope it helps you to awaken your own spirit of joy and power. First, you have to believe it is possible that a spirit of joy lives within you and wants you to be happy. It helps if you keep company with other happy people. It also helps if you can give and receive hugs and know someone loves you.

Try the suggestions from "Your Fairy Grandmother's Wake-Up Call." Take time to meditate, seeing your fairy grandmother in your mind's eye. Ponder your true heart's desire and the joy you feel when it is granted. Maybe you'll feel like singing. If you can't connect with your joy it is possible that your grief or anxiety is overwhelming. There are times in life when that happens. You may feel alone and helpless.

Rumi, the thirteenth-century Persian poet, refers to this despair in his poem, "Zero Circle."

> Be helpless, dumbfounded,
> Unable to say yes or no.
> Then a stretcher will come from grace
>   to gather us up.
> … miraculous beings come running to
>   help.

When I felt helpless, a fairy grandmother appeared as my miraculous being. I offer you her story in hopes that you, too, will find her or your own form of grace. The power is within. I trust you will find your own miraculous connection.

The next section, "Happily Ever After," can help you make that connection. "Your Fairy Grandmother's Wake-Up Call" will help you visualize your joyful spirit. "The Fairy Grandmother's Meditation" provides suggestions and bits of wisdom to contemplate and can stimulate memories of your own stories to help you discover your magic and create your happy endings. "The Reader's Guide" proposes questions for personal reflection and/or group discussion encouraging insightful conversation.

Happily Ever After

Your Fairy Grandmother's Wake-Up Call

*Y*ou can wake up your fairy grandmother within and welcome her into your life. She wants you to be happy.

Find a quiet time and place where you won't be disturbed. Take a moment to sit in the silence. Close your eyes, and take a deep breath. Breathe in and out slowly. Do that three times. In and out … in and out … in and out.

Picture your fairy grandmother in your mind's eye. You can *see* her. What does she look like? Someone you know or have seen before? A whimsical character? Your own special grandmother? A divine figure? This is *your* fairy grandmother within. She is smiling. She stands right in front of you, holding her magic wand. Ask her name. Ponder this moment.

"What is your true heart's desire?" she inquires softly. "Make a wish."

Keep your eyes closed. Make your wish. You will feel your fairy grandmother tap your head lightly with her wand.

"May your wish come true," she whispers. "May you find your true heart's desire."

Accept the blessing. Open your eyes and breathe. Step into your power.

Now, sing along with your fairy grandmother: "Fairy

tales can come true, it can happen to you, if you're young at heart."

Notice how happy you feel.

You are now empowered by your fairy grandmother. She will keep you young at heart. She is always available. Just close your eyes, and make a wish. Enjoy!

Fairy Grandmother's Meditation

Everyone has a fairy grandmother within, and everyone has stories. The purpose of this book is to introduce and awaken your fairy grandmother within, to spark you—the reader—into remembering your stories, to discover your magic, and to create happy endings.

These bits of wisdom from the fairy grandmother within and her delightful companions are offered for your consideration and contemplation.

1. Your fairy grandmother within, "Grants your true heart's desire and sparks joy."
2. Prince, the charming greyhound, shares his secret: "Love is stronger than death."
3. The Dandelion Fairy wants you to know, "Hope triumphs over experience."
4. Little Sunshine shares her joy: "To be heard is to be healed."
5. The magic wand helps you to take charge of your life: "Step into your power."
6. Grandma Mary Jo comes when called. She promises, "I'm always here for you."

7. Reader's wild card: Recall an incident from your life story that sparks joy.

Here's a recommended approach for your meditation.

Take your time. Study the list, pick one bit of magic, or let it pick you.

Read the sentence out loud three times.

Dwell on the thought that touches you.

Ask yourself what relevance or application this wisdom has for you.

Check the "Reader's Guide" for the quote you selected, and consider the questions for additional contemplation.

Savor the wisdom. Open yourself to whatever the message brings.

Let the message slowly seep into your being. Let this enchantment speak to your heart. Consider this moment. The fairy grandmother within reminds us to live in the moment. We only have this moment, this one precious moment.

Thank your fairy grandmother or your own divine grace for this meditation.

When you wake up tomorrow, it will be a new day and another opportunity to live, love, be happy, and to meditate. Pick another bit of magic you can savor from this list or another personal meditation.

Caution! Just select one bit of magic each day, or you may develop heartburn.

If you slip and forget a day, don't fret. When you recall your forgetting, pick yourself up, dust yourself off, and like the Dandelion Fairy, try again.

Moment by moment, day by day, you are composing your own story. Create it the way you want it.

Your fairy grandmother within sends her blessings. She stands ever ready to spark your heart with joy and help you step into your power. She is available 24-7. Don't hesitate to call.

Commit to memory, "I am never too old to be young at heart!"

Say it again: "I am never too old to be young at heart!"

Two fairy thumbs up!

Reader's Guide

This "Reader's Guide" is designed to help you use the stories in the book to awaken your spirit of joy, your fairy grandmother within.

When you are alone, ponder the questions on the following pages. If you can, it is more fun and profitable to share your reactions and ideas with another person or in a group.

Read the questions thoughtfully and without judgment. Answer them honestly. Don't let your inner critic or fear of what others might say or think hamper your truthful responses. The fairy grandmother within and her charming cast of characters have their own bits of wisdom that carry big magic. Take time to picture in your mind's eye each of the characters, and let them speak to your heart. Listen. Then let your heart speak to you.

Take time as you read the questions and think about your answers. Memories and old stories may emerge. Don't shut them down. Your may weep or laugh at past antics or sorrows. Shame or blame have no place now. They are no longer valid. You may want to seek or give forgiveness; it is always welcome.

The Hawaiian *Ho' oponopono* forgiveness ritual is very effective for asking or receiving forgiveness. Visualize the person you are addressing and repeat, "I'm sorry. Please forgive me. Thank you. I love you." You can also visualize this person repeating this message back to you. Accept the forgiveness and give thanks.

Each bit of magic appears on a separate page so you can make notes. Use separate paper if necessary.

1. Your fairy grandmother within: "Grants your true heart's desire and sparks joy."

   What is your true heart's desire?
   Are you ready to recognize your fairy grandmother within?
   How would that change your life?
   What sparks joy for you?

2. Prince, the charming greyhound. learned: "Love is stronger than death."

    Explore that idea for yourself. Do you believe it?
    What kind of love is stronger than death?
    Have you ever felt the presence or dreamed of a loved one who has crossed over?
    How did it feel? Did you talk about it with anyone?

3. The Dandelion Fairy believes: "Hope triumphs over experience."

    Do you believe in hope? Did you ever lose hope?
    Do you believe, "It is better to try and fail than never to have tried at all?"
    Did you ever make a mistake and fall on your fanny? Share if you dare.
    Did you ever pick yourself up and try again? And again?

4. Little Sunshine learned: "To be heard is to be healed."

   What does it mean, "To be heard"? Why is it so important?
   Do you feel that you have ever truly been heard? Do you feel that you hear others?
   What does it mean, "To be healed"?
   Is there a difference in being healed and being cured?

5. The magic wand helps you to take charge of your life: "Step into your power."

   What do you consider your power?
   What has kept you from claiming your power?
   What would happen if you stepped into your power today?
   Are you ready to be touched by the magic wand?

6. Grandma Mary Jo was available when needed. She says, "I'm always here for you."

   Is it important for you to have someone or something standing by?
   Is that someone or something available now?
   If not, what can you do to make it happen?
   Are you standing by for someone else?

7. Reader's Wild Card: Recall an incident from your life story. For example, a big moment—a wedding, birth of a child, loss of a loved one or pet, a simple encounter, or a dream.

   Does that story bring you joy or sorrow?
   Have you had a pet that you loved? Tell its story.
   Remember a special loved one. What brings the person back to your mind?
   How do you want to be remembered?

Resources

To learn more about the loving spirits of the older women (Council of Grandmothers) who share their blessings and empowerment and seek to bring healing balance back to our earth, check out www.grandmothersspeak.com or NetOfLight.org.

To learn more about the hospice nurses who offer hope and healing to veterans and their families, check out www.OpusPeace.org or www.Soulinjury.org.

To learn more about shamanism, check out the Foundation for Shamanic Studies website www.shamanism.org.

"Young at Heart" lyrics copyright Kobait Music Publishing Ltd.

Also by the author: *Thea, Spiritual Midwife––New Meaning to Life after Death*. Available on Amazon.com-books

About the Author

Jacqueline Thea, PhD, LMFT, is a licensed psychotherapist and dream counselor. She is a former professional guardian/conservator, registered nurse, and practitioner of harp therapy. She trained in shamanic studies.

Now in her late eighties, Thea celebrates life in Bend, Oregon, with loved ones and friends on both sides of the Rainbow Bridge. And like the fairies, Thea loves champagne and chocolate.